AF270624

Cavalier King Charles Spaniels

by Julie Murray

Abdo Kids Jumbo is an Imprint of Abdo Kids
abdobooks.com

abdobooks.com

Published by Abdo Kids, a division of ABDO, P.O. Box 398166, Minneapolis, Minnesota 55439.
Copyright © 2024 by Abdo Consulting Group, Inc. International copyrights reserved in all countries.
No part of this book may be reproduced in any form without written permission from the publisher.
Abdo Kids Jumbo™ is a trademark and logo of Abdo Kids.

Printed in the United States of America, North Mankato, Minnesota.

102023

012024

THIS BOOK CONTAINS
RECYCLED MATERIALS

Photo Credits: Getty Images, Shutterstock, Thinkstock

Production Contributors: Teddy Borth, Jennie Forsberg, Grace Hansen
Design Contributors: Candice Keimig, Pakou Moua

Library of Congress Control Number: 2023937667
Publisher's Cataloging-in-Publication Data

Names: Murray, Julie, author.

Title: Cavalier King Charles spaniels / by Julie Murray

Description: Minneapolis, Minnesota : Abdo Kids, 2024 | Series: Dogs | Includes online resources and
    index.

Identifiers: ISBN 9781098268510 (lib. bdg.) | ISBN 9781098269210 (ebook) | ISBN 9781098269562
    (Read-to-Me ebook)

Subjects: LCSH: Cavalier King Charles spaniel--Juvenile literature. | Toy dogs--Juvenile literature. | Dogs--
    Juvenile literature. | Dogs--Behavior--Juvenile literature. | Animal behavior--Juvenile literature.

Classification: DDC 599.772--dc23

Table of Contents

Cavalier King Charles Spaniels

Cavalier King Charles Spaniels are **companion** dogs. Their sweet faces and gentle manner make them a popular **breed**.

Cavalier King Charles Spaniels are **descendants** of English toy spaniels. English toys were **bred** in England as lap dogs. They kept **aristocrats** warm in cold castles and on carriage rides.

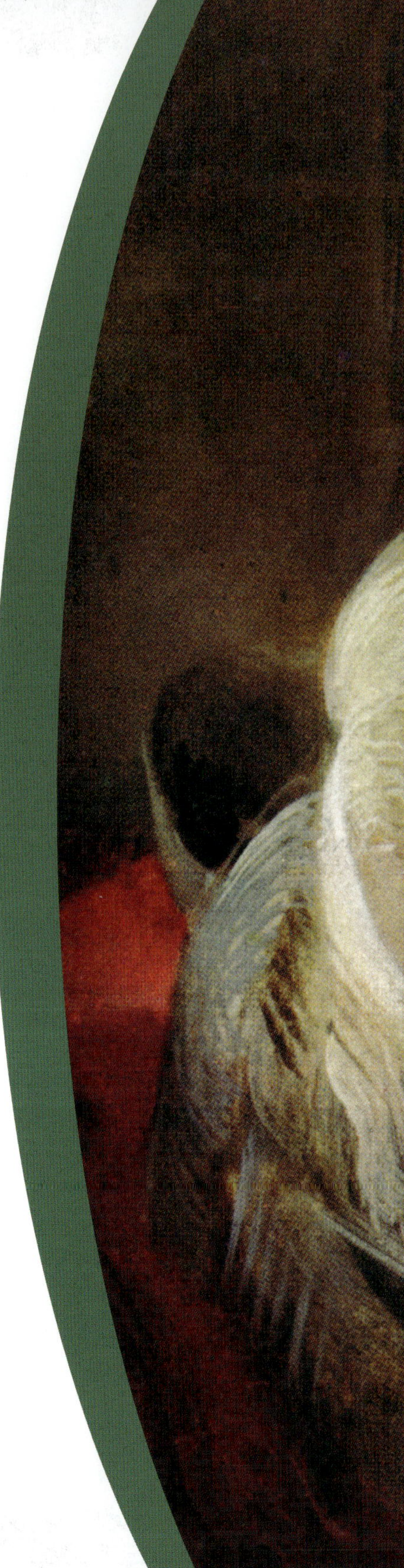

7

Cavaliers are small dogs. They

stand 13 inches tall (33 cm) and

weigh up to 18 pounds (8 kg).

They have large, round eyes

and long ears.

Their coats are long and silky. Coats come in four different color patterns. They are black-and-tan, ruby, Blenheim, and black-and-white.

ruby
black
and
white
Blenheim

Grooming

A Cavalier's silky coat should be brushed weekly. This will keep it healthy.

A Cavalier's floppy ears should be checked and cleaned regularly. The dog also needs its nails trimmed along with an occasional bath.

Exercise

Cavaliers are happy being lap dogs, but also enjoy the outdoors. A daily walk should satisfy their exercise needs.

Personality

Cavaliers are smart and easy to train. They are eager to please. Some do well in **agility training**.

Cavaliers are loving and loyal

dogs. They enjoy being around

their owners. They make great

family pets and get along well

with other animals.

21

More Facts

- King Charles II of England loved and helped breed English toy spaniels. The dogs were often called King Charles spaniels. In the early 1900s, people worked to breed dogs that more resembled the dogs King Charles II loved. This is how the Cavalier King Charles Spaniel was created.

- Cavaliers make great therapy dogs. They are also good dogs for older adults.

- The breed was officially recognized by the American Kennel Club in 1995.

Glossary

agility training – a type of exercise training that incorporates short bursts of movement that involve changes of direction.

aristocrat – a member of a small, privileged class known as the aristocracy; noble.

bred – developed over time for a certain purpose.

breed – a particular type of animal.

companion – one who spends time with another or others.

loyal – showing devotion and faithfulness to someone.

Index

Abdo Kids
ONLINE
FREE! ONLINE MULTIMEDIA RESOURCES

Visit **abdokids.com** to access crafts, games, videos, and more!

Use Abdo Kids code **DCK8510** or scan this QR code!